You Left Me In April

Copyright © 2022 Stephanie Donovan

Cover art by Stephanie Donovan.

Author website: stephdonovan.wixsite.com/home

Dedicated to –

No one
Not anymore
Except my own pain
Which faded long ago
And made me
A part of me
At least

1/24/16

I think I inhaled you
Which makes exhaling
That much harder to do
Instead of letting go
I want to hold on
The life
The breath of it all
Ever so tight in my chest
I want to hold on
To everything
That I know
I should let go of

1/24/16

Because I am here
Thinking about the
Whys
What ifs
How comes
And *don't knows*
I hold onto myself
So tightly
Latched shut
Covered up
That the only thing
I'm left with
Loneliness
In the dark
So why do I
Hold onto myself

1/24/16

You came in like the tide
Slowly
With ease
Then suddenly
All at once
And I ran for the sand
Tried to dry myself of your salt
But was only left with soggy hands
Covered in grit
Parching myself in the sun didn't help
Because all I could feel was your touch
On my toes
Sending shivers
Up my bones
I couldn't dry myself of you then

1/24/16

Jumping was hard
Not like walking
For that edge
I built it all up
Thought it all out
And only felt more anxious
For that shock
The bolt
The drop
In my stomach
Through my spine
Clearing my mind
And before I knew it
I landed
Both feet steady
Sturdy
And fine

1/24/16

And I don't know why
I feel like a fool
As high as the sky
I can do it if I try
But hands stained
Mind blurred
Soul mixed
Heart floating
Just boating through
Searching
Reaching for you
Seems conflicting
Yet worth something
(If only I knew)

1/24/16

Purple underwear
Unfaded dreams
Tangled fingers
Midnight please
Keep me up and make me tried
But never leave me
Uninspired
I want to melt
Alone
With you

1/24/16

Can I say
I can't help but feel like this
Wanting picnic trips and long car drives
Museum visits and park walks
Just long enough for us to talk
And dream
And wish
That life could always feel like this

1/24/16

Because all I want to hear you say
Is that everything will be okay
That you're worth it
And I deserve it
As selfish as that may be
I expect the best
For both you and me

1/24/16

So many things
Swirling though my head
Just can't seem to go to bed
I want you to know
That I yawn for attention
Stretch for perfection
Have little words
Yet still strive to talk
Tick goes my clock
Midnight already
But this air is still heavy
Hard as I may try
I can still manage to get by
With this weight
Waiting for a date
Hoping
Coping
That something
Might show me
The way
Someday

1/25/16

I want to make a tent along the beach
Claim land that isn't ours
Stay there for hours
Bath beneath the stars
I wouldn't wish for anything more
Than to be only yours

1/25/16

I think I wished
On my fair share of stars
Filled up my voucher
Can't use this card
So I wish on the little things
Road trips of spring
Beach rides of summer
Fogs in fall
The snow drifts of winter
All much closer to Earth
Less time to travel
Maybe then
I will get what I'm after

1/25/16

Like a memory is forever
So is your face
And I don't know
If you could ever be replaced
But my heart is a boat
Weathered and worn
And yours is a battle
Fevered and forlorn
Only time will tell
If I'll dock
If you'll stop
And we'll walk for a bit
Maybe sit down
Just talk
About mermaids and scars
I've seen the unbelievable
And you've done it all

1/25/16

Can I talk about flying
I really hope
For my soul is wired
And ready to bolt
I've come to the idea
That dreams do come true
And you may have noticed
That I've chosen you

1/26/16

Paint me black
Blend me in
Peaceful night
I'll let it in

1/27/16

I think about a blue house
A white cat
A speckled dog
Early mornings and tangled sheets
Hot breakfast and coffee needs
Short farewells
Lips caressing
Always know
That I'll be missing
The sight of you
The scent of you
Reminders you're here

1/29/16

I watched the moon glow tonight
And wondered if it was alive
Because just like it
I too can be bright
Then dim
And hide

1/29/16

Burry me in the dirt next to yours
Bring the rain
Let it pour
I want the earth
To have my skin
Let the world win
Deliver my flesh from where it came
I've been vain
But I won't keep it
Don't let a coffin hold my body
Earth and linen
Don't worry about the weather
Burry me with him
After all
Let us mix
Nature brought us together
Fate may have led us
But nature will do us in the end

1/29/16

In a land
So green and blue
I left it all with you
My hopes
My dreams
My feelings too
And I know it might seem
Too optimistic
I must admit it
But know I'm scared
To give you this bearing
But something tells me
Late at night
When the stars are bright
And you're not here
To twirl my hair
I just know
You'll hold my *everythings*
So tight
With much delight

2/1/16

I'm a mystery to many here
With my open book policy

2/3/16

Spin me a story
I hope you don't mind
Of two people together
And everything on their mind
They can't seem to break it
This thing that they share
Down stairs
Busted tables
And plenty of pulled hairs
But try as they might
They can't seem to get it
To bust it
To break it
No gluing back the pieces
Though oppress it
As they might
Things just come together
Like leaves in the fall
Like time with us all
And in the end
Who knows
How this story does go
You just believe in better endings
White winters
Never endings

2/3/16

I think running away
Would be a fine idea
Head not very clear
Pushing away that fear
Make the run
Take the plunge
Hold my hand
Squeeze me dry
Till I'm a puddle
Be by my side
Through all the weather
For the better
I'll never be blue
For I have you

2/4/16

I sit here wondering
Fan buzzing
Mind running
Heart racing
Soul chasing
About life outside of this
These walls that hold me
Land that parts us
I wonder if it's better
Even dryer
Maybe wetter
A little steeper
Possibly deeper
But if it has you
I'll crack walls with bare hands
Run over land with no shoes
To find my wandering
Wondering
Mind
With you

2/4/16

I've been afraid to fly
To crash
Burn
And die
I've been afraid to unlock
To peel
Break
Pick the lock
I've made a prison
Out of myself
Built the walls
Laid the concrete
No windows
No way out
I have come
To a break
Faking good times
Gone to waste
Precious tastes
No other way
So I'll kick and scream
Break the theme
So I'll cry all night
Never give up this fight
To pull down walls
Let go of it all
The fear
I'll conquer it
The plunge
I'll take it
I've been afraid
To unlock
It is about time
To stop
The clock

2/4/16

I forgot what you sounded like
And I was dying to remember
A fleeting shiver
I'm not too clever
But my words are few
And far from one another
I'm trying to make it seem
Like I have it all together
Stitched up memories

2/6/16

Can I compare you to a star
Because you're always so very far
Always bright as can be

2/7/16

He makes me paper-thin
How hard is it to ask
To make this last

2/7/16

Days go by
And I still cry
Dreams come by harder
And tears fall farther
Could be happy
I'm just too sappy
A dreamer
Believer
I wish
Not just for moments
I'll have broken
Good times, too

2/7/16

I call myself mental
But you call me yours
I can't help but adore
And ignore
Because I'm so unsure
Like a pain
It won't go away
So please
Never stop
Always flaunt
In calling me yours

2/9/16

So what
You want to leave
On your own
Go
Just know
I'll rob that scar you gave me
And mutter to myself
A thank you
Because you left something behind
That it was real
Thank you
Shaky hands write

2/13/16

I've written myself a tragedy
A story not to be told
And maybe I've exaggerated truths
But that's the way the truth is always told
So many people have left
And on their own accord
I don't know if it's because of me
Or just how the weather turns its course

2/14/16

Let me
Write a book
Paint a picture
Something for people to remember
Walk along the shore
Don't know what for
Kiss all night
Sleep the day away
Laughter and good tears
Watch you grow a beard
Call the ocean our own
Always have a home
In each other
Forever and ever
Till all the stars die
And our wishes are forgotten

2/16/16

What am I working towards
I've fallen behind
Can't pick it up
Or find the motivation
To keep myself going on
In a different situation
Was I meant to be like this?
Cold outside
Hot inner middle
Dripping through the days
Watching the world fade away
Or is this my limbo?
Have to spin the wheel myself
But a year later
Here I lay
Watching the world
Drip
Drop
Away

2/16/16

All I know is that I want you
A constant feeling
To be by my side
Even with the faces
That I hide

2/17/16

One could stab me from behind
And I would easily come running back

2/18/16

I carry dreams I shouldn't
The weight too great
So I must burry them
In a garden
Like a grave
One I'll have named
After you

2/20/16

I think I've wished far too hard
You don't seem to come true anymore
Not that I pleaded too hard before
But like a cool breeze in the spring
Parting air
Heading north without much care
You've left me in a bloom
Colorful
Yet too soon
To bake and ache
And wonder what it would take
For one more day of winter
To break this pain

2/22/16

Follow me to the ocean
I won't roam very far
You'll see me by the way
That I watch the stars

2/22/16

You're my own personal getaway
I'll never mind if you stay all day
Life's more beautiful when you're around
Pretty colors
Softer sounds
So let's lay in bed and never leave
Think of what we've always dreamed
I'd climb a mountain if I could
Write words that everyone understood
Make life a little sweeter
Minds a bit deeper
But changing others is a task
And not to sound down
But I have only found
That the one person
I'd never change
Is you
Dream it true
I'd spend all day with you

2/23/16

New horizons
I call for better days
New beginnings
Don't let me just slip away
New inspiration
Leave something to be desired
New day
Never be too far away

2/23/16

Kiss me in museums
Always hold my hand
Next to beautiful paintings
That will always have its' fans
Like them we are priceless
In this moment held together
By determined hearts
Steady hands
Better weather

2/23/16

Let's go where no one knows our faces
Pace streets with unfamiliar names
Spend a day looking lost in the rain
And at night
Hold me close
My happy place

2/23/16

I want you too much
This is all I know
Like a plant reaching for water
Just trying to grow
But springing from concrete
Is a hard task to do
As is holding onto you
Without feeling too blue
So please
Call me again
I need you
Constant
And in my head

2/23/16

Let me know
Every one of your scars
Stories that marred
And with this knowledge
I promise not to travel far
For lands may hold tales
Mysteries many
But I could spend a lifetime with you
Telling me how you got so many

2/23/16

Pleas just tell me
That's it's going to work out
Even though there's
A storm in my chest
Passion in my mind
Stars in my eyes
Your universe
My heart
Your adventure
And my mind
Your mess to make
Pathetic
It's true
But I think
Even more so
I want all of this
To be real
For me
With you

2/23/16

How is it
That you always make me this sad
This glad
Being with you is like rainy weather
Pour over me
But never make me wish for an umbrella
Even like this
I have never
Been better

2/27/16

You want to talk
This weather's dreary
You said
Give me a minute
I'm feeling weary
Just life
You know
I try to drive it fast
But then it takes me slow
And I can never know
Just which way to go
Will it take me 'round again?
But will it leave me before the end?
I never know
Just which way to go

3/3/16

I feel like I'm only existing
A realization that hurts the most
Because I thought that living
Was supposed to be
What I needed
To want
The most

3/8/16

I couldn't believe it
The loss that I felt
Because so much had been left
And nothing had ever been held
I had built perfection in my head
Nothing fancy
Just a roof
Close to the stars
And a beach
Not very far
I'd thought of travels to go
Animals to name
Conversations to be had
Some maybe in the rain
But that's where I went wrong
I hoped too hard for it all
Right from the start
I never had you at all

3/8/16

I can't look myself in the mirror
I've been such a fool
To think that I could believe
In someone as good as you
I wish my heart
My thoughts
My fire
Longed a little less
I wish life
Left me behind
Without such a mess

3/14/16

I fell for you in the snow
You didn't keep me all that warm
But even now
You've left me cold

3/15/16

I wanted you to leave me bruises and marks
Little reminders that you were once there
Just not these kind

You make me rumble
Tumble
Make my voice crumble
I keep it all inside
Where I hide

To get away
To spend a day

I can't let things go
This much I know

I could be happy
Not just in moments
But every single day
With you

Do you ever think that we're meant to be?
That everything we've worked for
Comes back to you
Maybe me

I may not have him
But at least I can dream him
It's bittersweet
Not usually a treat

I think you always
Must give some people
A little piece of you to eat
Chew
Destroy

I stripped away the petals
The thorns
I did not mind
For underneath
I knew there was beauty
Heavenly
Mine

You left me
An open book

Daydreaming
That's all I ever do
But not with you

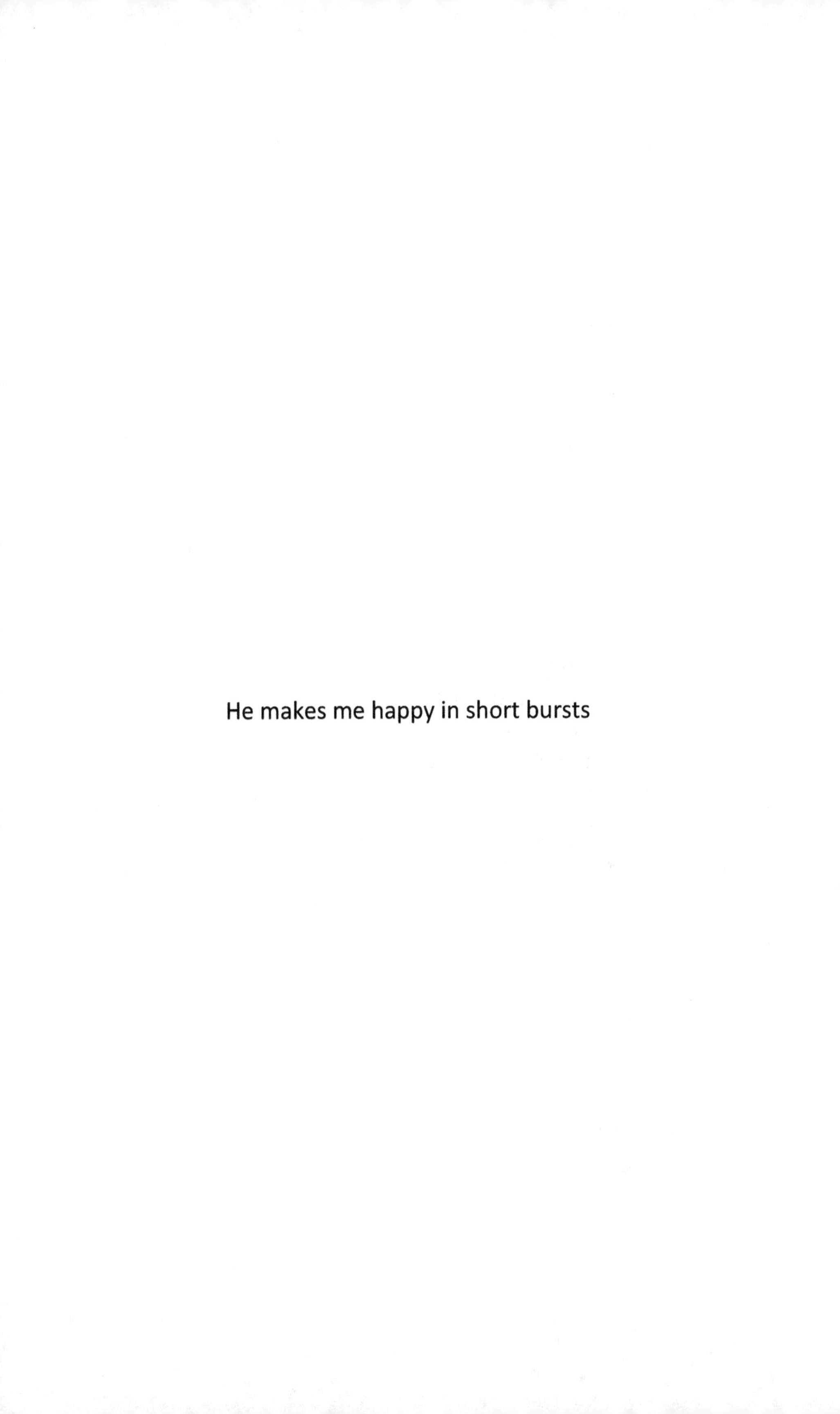

He makes me happy in short bursts

Isn't that sad of me
That I found happiness in someone
Who could easily leave
Live without me

I miss so much of that night
When I'm lonely and not so bright

10/16/2017

How long am I supposed to sit here and wait
For the words to sprout in my head
I need to go to bed
But I found a new angle
It's not at all simple
I won't say it aloud
For it will make me sound proud –

I'd rather hop on a plane
See a different ocean
Remember a friend
Never give up my devotion
For finding my own breath
My own calm
Amongst myself

And when I need to
At times
I take a look on a shelf
Where I've stored all my memories
Lessons
Reasons galore
And one book
Somewhat dusty
Has your name written on it
I never say it out loud
Not anymore
I still won't
As I type this
Head wondering why
A goodbye was never given
Only the sentiment of
You had tried
I'd forgiven

But now that I've read back
This is a girl I still know
Who discovered
Life never turns out
Just quite how you imagine
And maybe that's why
This burn in my throat still arises

Lonely winter
I would not change you
Even if I could
Just make you listen
Understand
What I've come to know

If I had to take it back
I'm not sure I'd spoil it
For you left me with long days
Silly questions
Little rhythms
But defiantly not reason

I want to close this book now
Not look at it for days
Find solace in myself
And plenty of new days
Remember when we said
It'd be forever and ever
I'm taking it back now
It should have been then
And then never

I still don't understand
Why it makes me so blue
To think about what if
I could have been with you
But a promise is made
To be kept intact
And your words were like knives
And I couldn't tape those pieces back

So you and I
Are not now
Or then
Not today
And never again
Always

That door
I still shut it
On days when it's warm
But nights
When I'm chilly
I release hinges
Witness storms

Take me as you may
Future ventures
Souls I still have yet to meet
For I come from cold weather
A chill that can't be beat

And don't give me the pity
Some may desire
I've realized if you live
Then spark fires
Don't need a lighter

But as I take this lost moment
A time that never was
And place it back on the shelf
Not a speck of dust
I think of that April
The one before last
And I'm at least grateful
I had myself
To forgive
Hopefully laugh at

So give me more things
To collect on this shelf
Maybe not an April
Just little lessons
Small thoughts
On how to treat myself
Maybe get lost
Because life was made
To be followed
Trailed by lines
And dots

So I lost you in April
All this has been true
And my mind is still weary
Thinking of you
But I like learning morals
As hard as they may seem
Because I grow into a person
That now I only dream

Still clumsy
And foolish
Oh, I had this one coming
But what's a life without shelves
In need of some dusting

16 July 2021

I laugh
At my kind sadness
Young girl
This was too much
For a boy who wasn't worth it
And with a heart
You couldn't even touch

I was right
About one thing
Life –
This ride
It does go on
And if I don't
Ride the waves
I'll find myself
Lost

2/20

I will take all of my pain

And cascade it out into the universe

I no longer want to bear it

These things others do to me

I react with such disdain

So take your own pain

And plant its seeds in someone else's garden

Mine is full

Stephanie Donovan is an author and poet from Boston, Massachusetts. She began writing poetry from a young age – a habit that has continued through to her adulthood, as a way to feel, cope, and escape. When she is not writing, Donovan is continuing her studies in communications and writing towards her bachelor's degree. *You Left Me In April* is her debut collection of poetry.